NATIONAL
GEOGRAPHIC
KiDS

weird but true! 4

350 OUTRAGEOUS FACTS

NATIONAL GEOGRAPHIC
WASHINGTON, D.C.

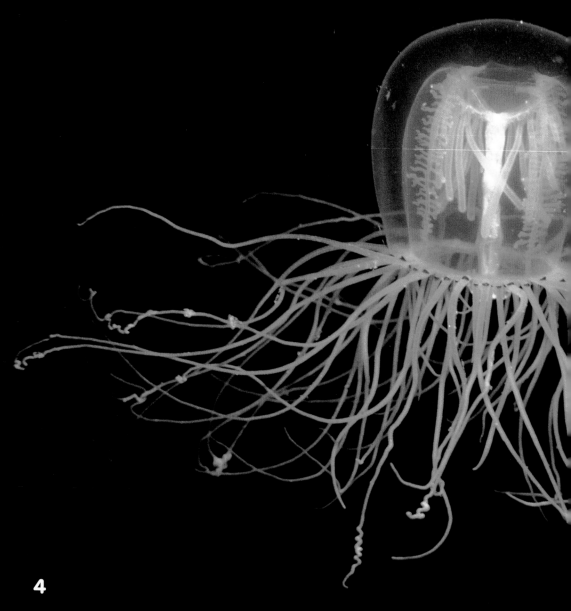

4

Some jellyfish glow.

THERE'S A MUSHROOM NAMED AFTER SPONGEBOB SQUAREPANTS.

Deep-fried **Kool-Aid** is sold as a snack at a county fair in California, U.S.A.

LEMONS CAN **POWER** LIGHTBULBS.

A man skipped a rock on water **51** times in one throw.

The last thing **Elvis ate** was **ice cream** and **cookies.**

MILLIONS OF YEARS AGO, **THERE WAS A BIRD** IN AUSTRALIA THAT WEIGHED AS MUCH AS A **POLAR BEAR.**

More earthquakes occur in Alaska than in any other U.S. state.

Fire trucks were originally painted

The death's-head **moth** has a **skull-shaped design** on its body.

red because that was the cheapest color.

Teams of **soccer-playing** robots compete every year at the **RoboCup.**

MUSICIANS PERFORMED A HIGH-FREQUENCY **ROCK CONCERT** IN AUSTRALIA THAT **ONLY DOGS COULD HEAR.**

A HORSE NEVER BREATHES THROUGH ITS MOUTH, EXCEPT IN EMERGENCIES.

Ants
AS BIG AS THIS TOY CAR ONCE MARCHED ON EARTH.

Hummingbird **nests** are about the size of a **golf ball.**

Laid end to end, all of the **iPhones** and **iPads** SOLD in one year would STRETCH around the **Earth.**

There's a condition that makes it impossible for some people to recognize faces.

The average strawberry has 200 seeds.

No red **M&M's** were produced between 1976 and 1987.

BOX JELLYFISH HAVE EYES BUT NO BRAIN.

ANTARCTICA HAS 24 HOURS OF DAYLIGHT FOR PART OF THE SUMMER.

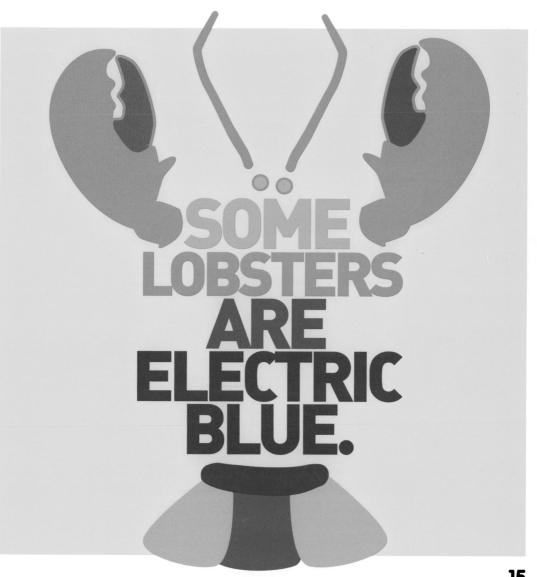

SOME LOBSTERS ARE ELECTRIC BLUE.

Your hands have

26 percent of the bones
in your body.

There are 27 bones
in each hand,

including your wrist.

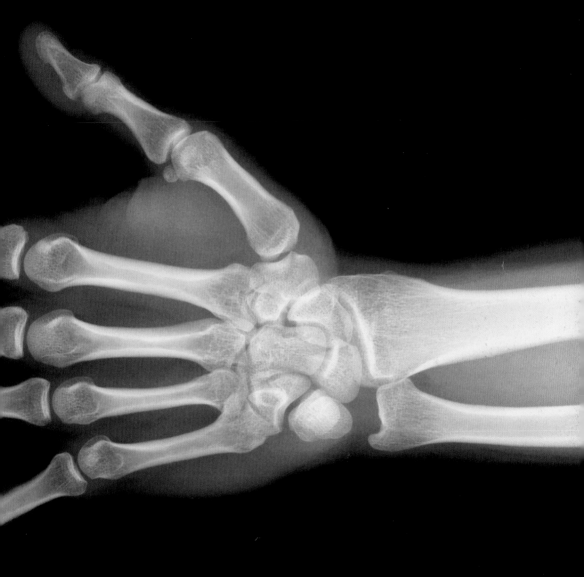

TERMITES EVOLVED FROM COCKROACHES.

GIRLS SEND AND RECEIVE MORE THAN TWICE AS MANY TEXT MESSAGES AS BOYS.

Competitors race tricked-out **portable potties** at the annual **outhouse races** in Nevada, U.S.A.

Some Ice Age people used **human skulls** as drinking **cups.**

Russian supermarkets carry **caviar-flavored** potato chips.

The **moon** can look red during a **lunar eclipse.**

The first **stop signs** were **black and white.**

The Frisbee was originally named the Pluto Platter.

IF A SPACE SHUTTLE COULD TRAVEL TO THE SUN IT WOULD TAKE ABOUT 228 DAYS TO GET THERE.

THERE'S AN ANNUAL REDHEAD FESTIVAL IN THE NETHERLANDS.

SOME CHICKENS ARE BORN HALF MALE, HALF FEMALE.

21

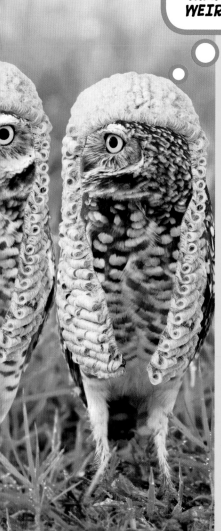

A
group
of
owls
is called a
parliament.

Some **bats'** hearing is strong enough to detect the sound of a beetle walking on a leaf.

Some cave-dwelling **salamanders** don't have **eyes.**

PREHISTORIC HUMANS **CHEWED** TREE RESIN AS CHEWING GUM.

THE LONGEST NONSTOP FLIGHT BY A BIRD IS **200 DAYS.**

A pair of ruby slippers from *The Wizard of Oz* sold for more than $660,000.

THE UNIVERSE IS FLAT.

More than
5 billion
green
**Monopoly
houses**
have been
manufactured
since the
game
was introduced
in 1935.

A white stork in Germany mysteriously turned blue.

There are about
three pounds
of bacteria (1.4 kg)
living in your stomach.

BEES CAN SEE ULTRAVIOLET, YELLOW, BLUE, AND BLUE-GREEN, BUT NOT RED.

Each year about

1,000,000,000,00

000,000,000,000
snow crystals
drop from the sky.

Some **gorillas play tag.**

TAG, YOU'RE IT!

It's possible for a **seed** to blow across **the ocean** and **sprout** on another **continent.**

New Caledonian **crows** make right-handed and left-handed **tools.**

Coughing while you get a shot can make it hurt less.

MOST BATS CAN'T TAKE FLIGHT FROM THE GROUND.

A dog named **Yoda** won the World's Ugliest Dog Contest.

A BEAVER
COULD SWIM 16 LAPS
IN AN OLYMPIC-SIZE POOL
WITHOUT TAKING A BREATH.

CRABS ARE DISTANT RELATIVES OF SPIDERS.

LAS VEGAS, *Nevada, U.S.A.,* **IS THE BRIGHTEST SPOT ON EARTH.**

The largest known **snowflake** was wider than a Frisbee.

THERE'S **A WINGLESS** ANT THAT CAN GLIDE FOR UP TO **90 FEET.** (27 m)

A speck of **blood** contains about **5 million red** blood cells.

can live for more than 100 years.

A FAMILY OF FIVE RODE A
FIVE-SEAT BIKE
6,439 MILES
(10,363 km)
FROM KENTUCKY TO ALASKA, U.S.A.,
IN ONE YEAR.

COMPETITORS HURL THEIR OLD
CELL PHONES
FOR SPORT AT FINLAND'S
MOBILE PHONE THROWING CHAMPIONSHIPS.

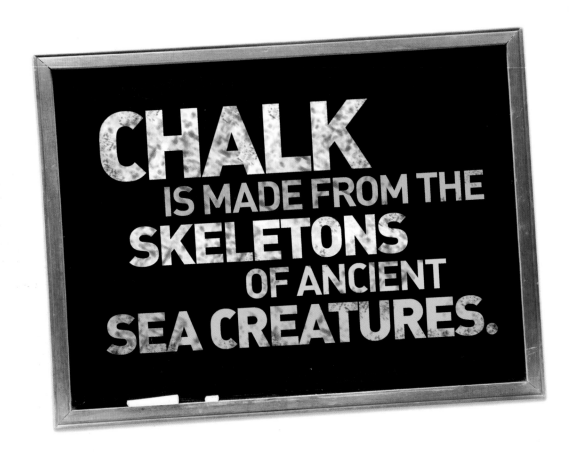

CHALK IS MADE FROM THE SKELETONS OF ANCIENT SEA CREATURES.

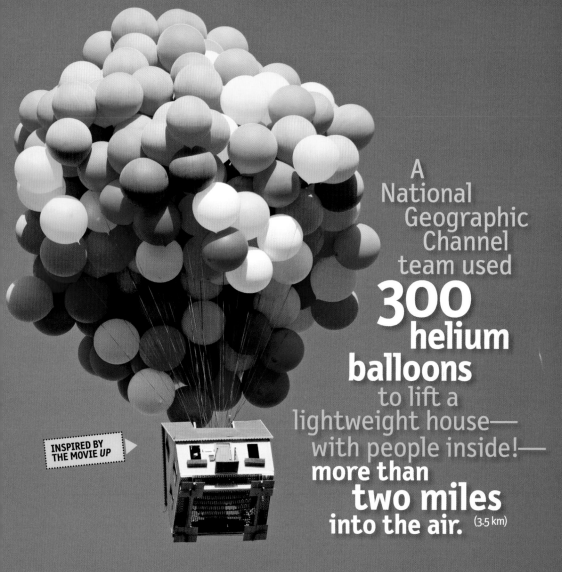

INSPIRED BY THE MOVIE *UP*

A National Geographic Channel team used **300 helium balloons** to lift a lightweight house— with people inside!— **more than two miles into the air.** (3.5 km)

AN OCTOPUS HAS RECTANGULAR PUPILS.

When there's thunder during a snowstorm, it's called

THUNDER-SNOW.

Odontophobia
is the fear of teeth.

You can beat **brain freeze** by pressing your tongue to the roof of your **mouth.**

U.S. DOLLARS ARE MADE OF COTTON AND LINEN, NOT PAPER.

Catfish have **ten times** more taste buds than people do.

SCIENTISTS DESIGNED **A ROBOTIC "EEL"** THAT DETECTS **POLLUTION IN WATER.**

INVENTED A HELMET "STEER" their parents. A New York, U.S.A., company that lets kids riding piggyback

CANADA minted a **GLOW-IN-THE-DARK COIN** for its **150th** anniversary.

JUNE 30 IS **ASTEROID DAY.**

The lower the sun is in the sky, the higher the rainbow.

IN BASEBALL, the phrase **"HITTING A CAN OF CORN"** refers to **CATCHING A ROUTINE FLY BALL.**

A REPAIRMAN **trapped in a cash machine** was rescued by **sending notes to customers** along with their receipts.

SHORT-TAILED WEASELS PERFORM **ELABORATE DANCES** to mesmerize rabbits.

There's a **FULL-SCALE REPLICA** of the **GREEK PARTHENON** in **NASHVILLE, TENNESSEE, U.S.A.**

Old English sheepdog + poodle = **sheepadoodle**

That's Weird!

SCIENTISTS HAVE CREATED **A LASER** THAT'S **ONE BILLION TIMES** BRIGHTER THAN OUR SUN.

A **RACOON** in FLORIDA, U.S.A., broke into a PARKED CAR **TO GIVE BIRTH.**

PENGUIN
DROPPINGS
CAN BE
pink.

YOU **GROW** FASTER IN
THE SUMMER THAN
YOU DO IN THE **FALL**.

There's a
fruit named
"stinking"
toe.

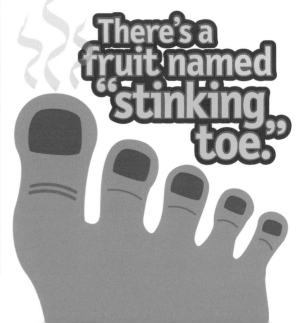

Elephants can swim for up to

6

hours without resting.

Some **sunspots**— magnetic fields on the sun— are bigger than **Earth.**

OUNCE FOR OUNCE, SOME **CATERPILLAR MEAT** CONTAINS **MORE PROTEIN** THAN **LEAN BEEF.**

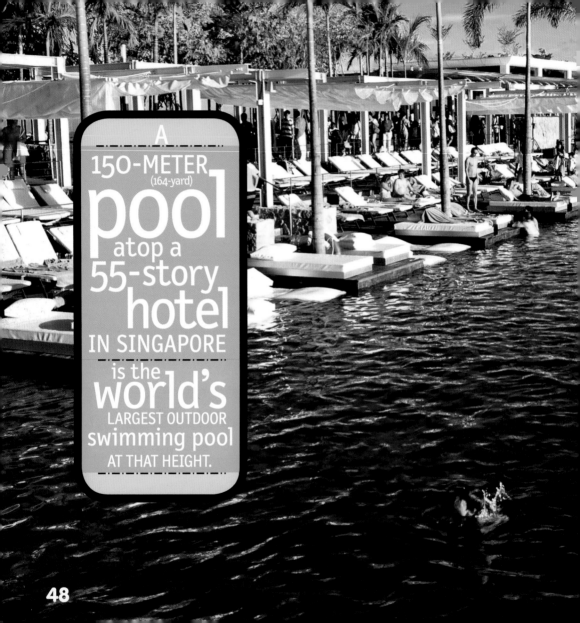

A **150-METER** (164-yard) **pool** atop a **55-story hotel** IN SINGAPORE is the **world's** LARGEST OUTDOOR **swimming pool** AT THAT HEIGHT.

Cockleshells are heart-shaped.

A narwhal's tusk tooth grows through its upper lip.

Ripe bananas glow blue under a black light.

A **MONTH** ON VENUS IS LONGER THAN A **DECADE** ON VENUS.

EVERY **BASEBALL** USED IN A MAJOR LEAGUE GAME GETS RUBBED DOWN WITH **MUD** BEFORE THE GAME.

Bats' knees face backward.

IT TAKES
THOUSANDS OF YEARS
FOR LIGHT
TO TRAVEL FROM THE
SUN'S CORE
TO ITS SURFACE.

If you could **drive to the sun,** it would take about **190 years** to get there.

The moon weighs 81,000,000,000,000,000,000 tons.

(73,000,000,000,000,000,000 t)

WATERMELONS ARE 92% WATER.

-40°F -40°C

-40° is the only temperature that is the same in Celsius and Fahrenheit.

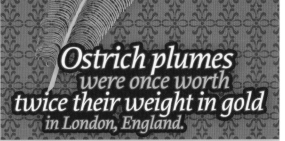

A WOODPECKER
CAN PECK A TREE
UP TO 30 TIMES A SECOND.

Ostrich plumes were once worth twice their weight in gold in London, England.

A bridge built in Lima, Peru, is reportedly held together by **egg whites**.

More than **950** beetles can live in a sloth's fur at one time.

You are **rarely** more **than** **six feet** (1.8 m) away from a **spider.**

THE WORLD'S **MOST** STOLEN FOOD IS CHEESE.

YOUR SKIN SHEDS AND REGROWS ONCE A MONTH.

An astronaut once lost a **SPATULA** during a space walk.

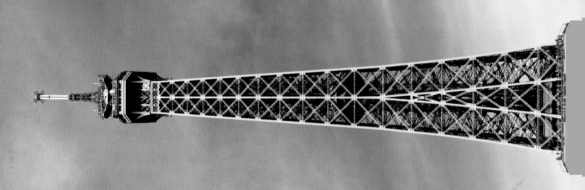

THE EIFFEL TOWER GETS REPAINTED EVERY SEVEN YEARS.

A man wrote an entire novel without using the letter "e."

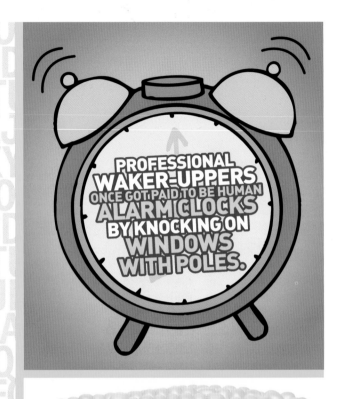

PROFESSIONAL WAKER-UPPERS ONCE GOT PAID TO BE HUMAN ALARM CLOCKS BY KNOCKING ON WINDOWS WITH POLES.

There is almost always an even number of rows on an ear of corn.

Many astronauts crave Tabasco sauce in space.

PIRANHAS BARK.

Sound travels 15 times faster through steel than through air.

SOME SPIDERS SPIN WEBS

2012

Some musicians with amnesia can still remember how to play music.

2020

LONGER THAN TWO CITY BUSES!

A GROUP OF
TURKEYS

TOADS DO NOT HAVE TEETH.

THE SPATULA-TAILED
HUMMINGBIRD'S
TAIL IS SO HEAVY
THAT IT CAN ONLY FLY
FOR A FEW SECONDS.

ONE OF JUPITER'S MOONS,
CALLED EUROPA,
MAY HAVE TWICE AS MUCH WATER
AS ALL THE OCEANS ON EARTH.

SOME MAMMAL SPECIES GROW BIGGER
IN COLD CLIMATES.

The first person arrested for speeding in the United States was driving **12 miles an hour** in 1899. (19 km/h)

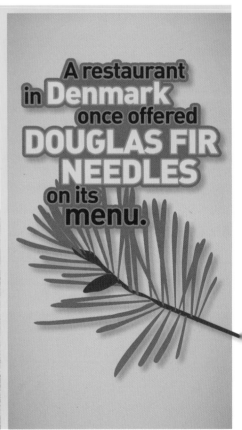

A restaurant in **Denmark** once offered **DOUGLAS FIR NEEDLES** on its menu.

A kangaroo **rat** does not need to **drink water.**

THERE'S ENOUGH PAINT ON THE WORLD'S LARGEST PASSENGER JET TO COVER TEN BASKETBALL COURTS.

There is a **trap** designed to catch **Bigfoot** in a **forest** in Oregon, U.S.A.

THE WORLD'S FASTEST TYPIST CAN REACH SPEEDS OF 200 WORDS PER MINUTE.

Porcupine **quills** were once used as toothpicks.

A puppy in California, U.S.A., was so tiny it was smaller than an iPhone!

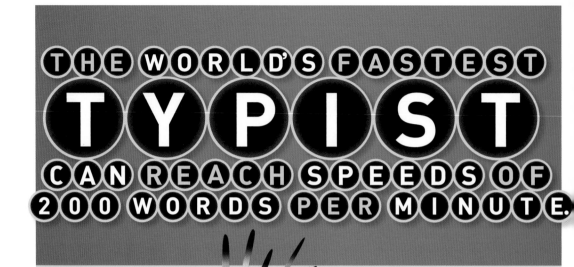

AT TWO WEEKS OLD

THE ENERGY IN
**ONE BOLT OF
LIGHTNING**
COULD TOAST ABOUT
100,000
SLICES OF BREAD.

AFGHANISTAN AND **AZERBAIJAN** ARE THE ONLY COUNTRIES THAT BEGIN, BUT DON'T END, WITH THE **LETTER A.**

90 percent of an **iceberg** is **underwater.**

A TEENAGER CREATED A **STAPLE CHAIN** THAT'S AS LONG AS A CRUISE SHIP.

There are more than twice as many chickens on Earth as people.

Moviemakers invented a new language for the made-up **Na'vi people** in the movie *Avatar.*

Snail slime can be used to soften skin.

Some **wasps** use pebbles as hammers to build their nests.

STOMACH ACID CAN DISSOLVE METAL.

NASCAR **DRIVERS** CAN LOSE **5 TO 10** (2.3 to 4.5 kg) **POUNDS IN SWEAT** DURING ONE RACE.

There's a beach in the Bahamas where you can swim with wild pigs.

Eleven

miles an hour is the (17.7 km/h) **fastest** a vehicle has ever driven on the **moon—** that's about as fast as you ride a bike!

CANADA'S POSTAL CODE FOR THE NORTH POLE IS HOH OHO.

Santa Claus
North Pole
HoH OHO
Canada

SOME PREHISTORIC PEOPLE USED MAMMOTH BONES TO BUILD THEIR HOMES.

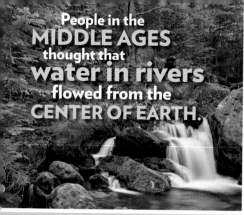

People in the **MIDDLE AGES** thought that **water in rivers** flowed from the **CENTER OF EARTH.**

A FIVE-FOOT (1.5-M) **GIANT SHIPWORM** THAT LIVES NEAR UNDERSEA HYDROTHERMAL VENTS **"EATS" CHEMICALS.**

The **SLOWEST SUNSETS** happen around the **SUMMER AND WINTER SOLSTICES.**

A MAN in California, U.S.A., **ROBBED A CELL PHONE** store **WEARING SOCKS** on his **HANDS.**

PEANUT BUTTER CAN **MOISTURIZE HAIR.**

In French text lingo, **"LOL"** is **"MDR,"** for *mort de rire,* which means **"DYING OF LAUGHTER."**

NEW YORK CITY'S BROOKLYN BRIDGE has **14,060** miles (22,627 km) of wire— that's longer than twice the distance from London to Hong Kong.

The MACY'S THANKSGIVING DAY PARADE includes about **1,000 CLOWNS.**

A BRITISH ARTIST created a **26-foot** (8-m) **tall** sculpture out of **FOUR TONS** (3.6 t) of **RECYCLED COMPUTER PARTS.**

A man from Punjab, India, set a **NEW WORLD RECORD** by spinning a **BASKETBALL ON TOP OF A TOOTHBRUSH** he held in his mouth FOR NEARLY A MINUTE.

That's Weird!

A CENTIPEDE discovered in **SOUTHEAST ASIA CAN RUN UNDERWATER.**

EYELASH VIPER EGGS
hatch inside their **MOTHER'S BODY.**

A
giant
anteater
is
6 feet
long, (1.8 m)
yet its
mouth
is as small
as a grape.

FUNGUS CAN GROW OUT OF A ZOMBIE ANT'S HEAD.

EWW, FUNGUS!

One gold coin sold for a whopping $7.4 million.

In Japan, the "OK" sign means "Pay me."

IT TAKES A **WET DOG** LESS THAN A **SECOND** TO SHAKE OFF **HALF** OF THE **WATER** ON ITS FUR.

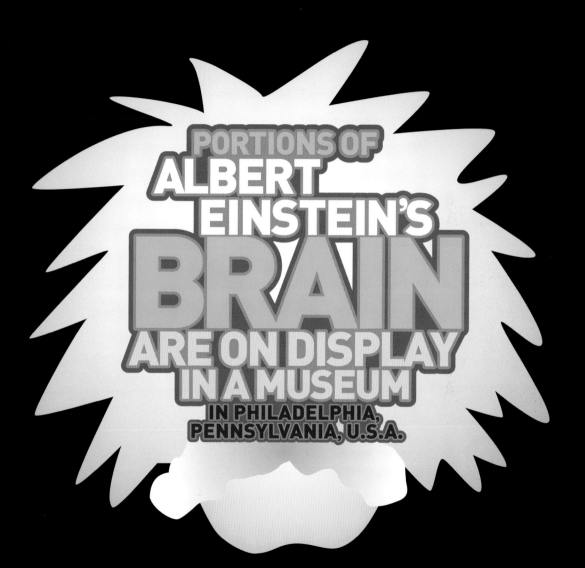

PORTIONS OF **ALBERT EINSTEIN'S BRAIN** ARE ON DISPLAY IN A MUSEUM IN PHILADELPHIA, PENNSYLVANIA, U.S.A.

Tasmanian **devils** sometimes **sneeze** to challenge other devils to a fight.

A FASHION **DESIGNER** CREATED A NEW **FABRIC** MADE ENTIRELY FROM **MILK.**

Silly Putty was used aboard **Apollo 8** to keep tools **from floating** around the ship.

TOOTHPASTE WAS ONCE MADE FROM **CUTTLEFISH BONES.**

THE FASTEST IS 4.73 SECONDS; A PERSON HAS EVER SOLVED A RUBIK'S CUBE A ROBOT DID IT MORE THAN FOUR SECONDS FASTER.

THE 100 YEARS' WAR

ACTUALLY LASTED 116 YEARS

(from 1337 to 1453).

A LUMP OF **GOLD** SMALL ENOUGH TO HOLD IN YOUR **HAND** CAN BE FLATTENED INTO A **SHEET** AS BIG AS A **TENNIS COURT.**

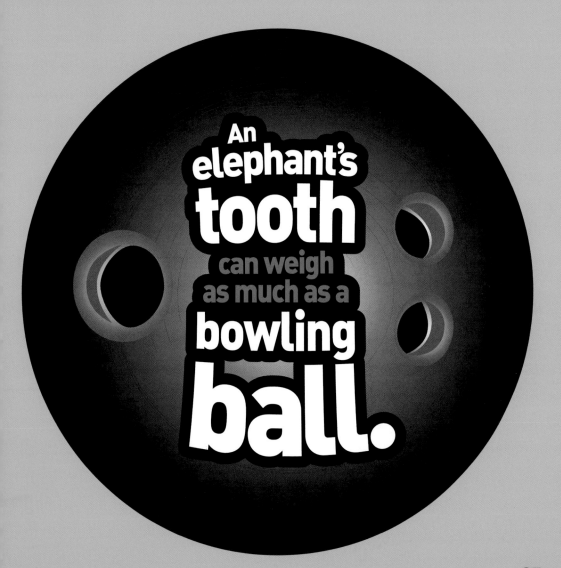

During the rainy season, **the water spilling over Africa's Victoria Falls** could fill **1,635 Olympic-size swimming pools** in one hour.

THE WORLD'S LONGEST

BEAVER DAM

IS ABOUT AS LONG AS 60 SCHOOL BUSES LINED UP END TO END.

The average **cherry tree** produces enough **fruit** every year to fill **28 pies.**

DUCT TAPE HAS BEEN USED TO REMOVE A WART.

▲
DON'T TRY THIS AT HOME!

Buttons were once made from **mussel shells.**

THE BRAIN DOESN'T FEEL PAIN.

There is a toilet museum in South Korea shaped like a toilet bowl.

CROCODILES SWALLOW ROCKS TO HELP DIGEST THEIR FOOD.

PEOPLE IN **SCOTLAND** USED TO CURE **BUTTER** BY **BURYING** IT IN **PEAT BOGS** FOR **SEVEN YEARS.**

MILLIONS OF YEARS AGO, AUSTRALIA'S DESERTS WERE AS WET AND LUSH AS A RAIN FOREST.

It can take up to three weeks to make a **Jelly Belly** *jelly bean.*

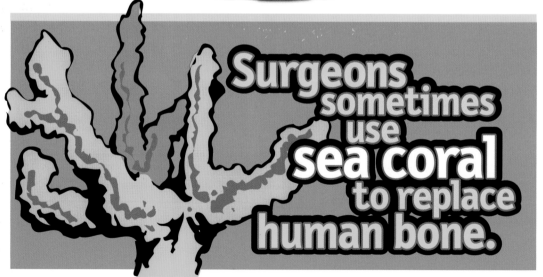

Surgeons sometimes use sea coral to replace human bone.

A STUDY FOUND THAT **DAIRY COWS** MAY PRODUCE MORE **MILK** WHILE LISTENING TO **CLASSICAL MUSIC.**

TWO TEENAGERS **LAUNCHED** A LEGO MAN **85,000 FEET** (25,900 m) INTO **SPACE** USING A **HOMEMADE WEATHER BALLOON.**

A **mouse** can squeeze through a **hole** the **size** of a piece of popcorn.

ASTRONAUT ALAN SHEPARD HIT **GOLF BALLS WHILE ON THE MOON.**

DOLPHINS EVOLVED FROM EARLY ANCESTORS OF GIRAFFES AND CAMELS.

PEOPLE IN THE
UNITED STATES
EAT MORE
BANANAS
THAN
APPLES
AND ORANGES
COMBINED.

PEOPLE IN THE
UNITED STATES
EAT MORE
BANANAS
THAN
APPLES
AND ORANGES
COMBINED.

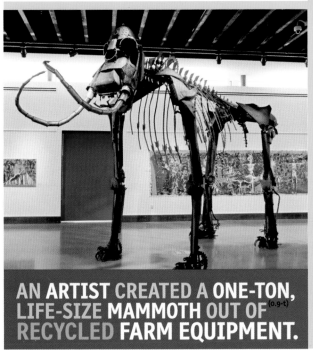

AN **ARTIST** CREATED A **ONE-TON,** LIFE-SIZE **MAMMOTH** OUT OF (0.9-t) RECYCLED **FARM EQUIPMENT.**

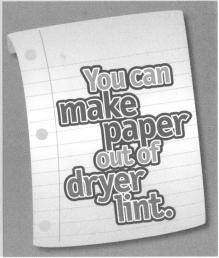

You can make paper out of dryer lint.

109

The Statue of Liberty's **torch** sways up to **5 inches** (12.7 cm) in the wind.

Artists in Italy created a pink stuffed **rabbit** big enough to see from space!

Wearing blue-tinted sunglasses may make you less hungry.

SCIENTISTS **FOUND A ONE-EYED "CYCLOPS" SHARK** IN MEXICO.

Most household **dust** contains dead skin.

After **recycling** almost all of their waste, **one family of four** was able to fit **a year's worth of trash** in a spaghetti sauce jar.

Pumice
is the
only rock
that can
float in water.

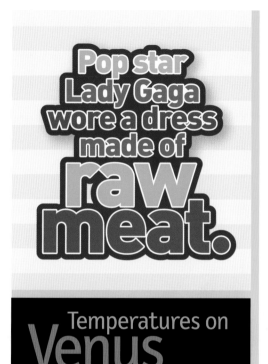

Pop star **Lady Gaga** wore a dress made of **raw meat.**

Temperatures on **Venus** reach more than (471°C) **880°F.**

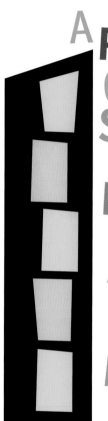

A **RAT** CAN **SURVIVE** A **FALL** FROM A **FIVE-STORY** BUILDING.

YOU MAY MAKE BETTER DECISIONS **WITH A FULL BLADDER.**

A
7-foot-9-inch
(2.1-m)
basketball
player
can
dunk
without
jumping.

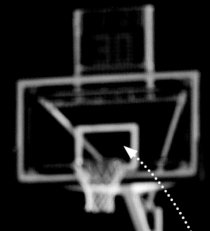

THE RAINIEST PLACE
IN THE CONTINENTAL UNITED STATES
—ABERDEEN, WASHINGTON—
GETS **11 FEET**
OF RAIN (3.4 m)
EVERY YEAR.
IF IT FELL ALL AT ONCE,
THE WATER WOULD BE ABOUT
4 FEET (1.2 m) HIGHER THAN A BASKETBALL HOOP.

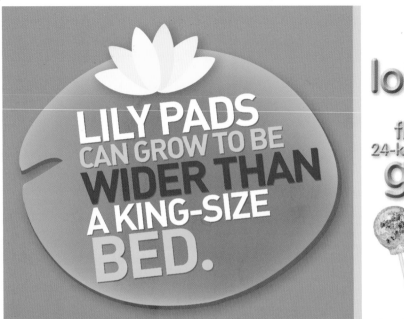

LILY PADS CAN GROW TO BE **WIDER THAN** A KING-SIZE **BED.**

You can buy **lollipops** made with flecks of real 24-karat **gold.**

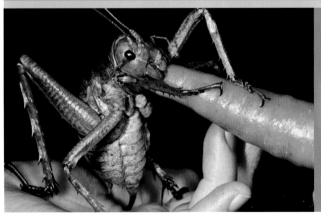

THE WORLD'S HEAVIEST INSECT, THE **giant weta,** IS BIG ENOUGH TO **EAT A CARROT.**

WHEN A KID LOSES A **TOOTH** IN GREECE, **HE THROWS IT ON THE ROOF!**

THE WORLD'S **RICHEST MAN** IS WORTH MORE THAN **$85 billion—** that's enough to buy a fleet of a million sports cars.

Every 50 years, rocks from Mars fall to Earth.

LEECHES CAN BE USED TO PREVENT BLOOD CLOTS.

Tomatoes were once thought to be poisonous.

Strawberry- and chocolate-covered Cheetos WERE SOLD IN JAPAN.

WALKING USES 200 MUSCLES.

A CUDDLY ROBOT HAS BEEN USED IN EXPERIMENTS TO CHEER UP LONELY PEOPLE.

A CAR COULD DRIVE AROUND EARTH **87 TIMES** ON THE AMOUNT OF FUEL IT TAKES TO FILL A JUMBO JET'S TANK.

Some **Greenland** **sharks** may live to be **200** years old.

Some **JUMPING SPIDERS** will chase **LASER POINTERS.**

THERE IS NO LOCAL TIME ZONE AT THE NORTH POLE.

Some **GOLF SHOTS** are known as **"BANANA BALLS"** for their **CURVING PATHS.**

There's a village named **GIGGLESWICK** in **NORTH YORKSHIRE, ENGLAND.**

Sunflowers can remove radioactive material from the soil they're planted in.

AN **ICEBERG** ABOUT THE SIZE OF DELAWARE, U.S.A., **BROKE OFF ANTARCTICA** IN 2017.

Researchers found a **3,000-YEAR-OLD PROSTHETIC BIG TOE** in an **Egyptian tomb**— the oldest artificial body part found so far.

HORSEY McHORSEFACE IS A **THOROUGHBRED RACEHORSE** from Australia.

AN APP can notify you when **YOUR CAT ENTERS AND LEAVES** through a pet door.

The fossil of a **110-MILLION-YEAR-OLD DINOSAUR** was **DISCOVERED** by a **SHOVEL OPERATOR** in a Canadian mine.

Some **PINEAPPLES** are **PINK INSIDE.**

That's Weird!

All the concrete used in a year could create an **89-FOOT** (27-m)- **HIGH WALL** around the **EQUATOR.**

Every **GIRAFFE** has a **unique COAT PATTERN.**

ONE OF THE WORLD'S LARGEST

ICEBERGS

IS BIGGER THAN NEW YORK CITY, U.S.A.

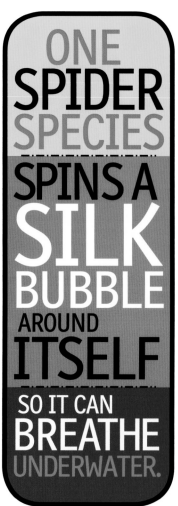

ONE **SPIDER** SPECIES SPINS A **SILK** BUBBLE AROUND **ITSELF** SO IT CAN **BREATHE** UNDERWATER.

"TWITCHERS" ARE PEOPLE WHO TRAVEL AROUND THE GLOBE TO SEE RARE BIRDS.

Most **frogs** eat their skin after they shed it.

THERE ARE NO COFFEE SHOPS IN A TOWN CALLED **HOT COFFEE,** IN MISSISSIPPI, U.S.A.

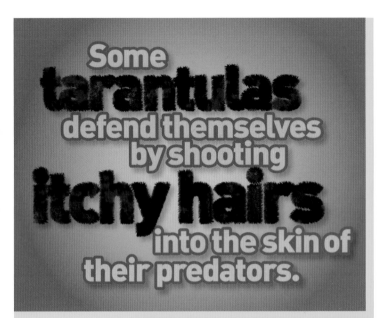

Some **tarantulas** defend themselves by shooting **itchy hairs** into the skin of their predators.

PEOPLE CAN BE ALLERGIC TO THE COLD.

The average **hug** lasts three seconds.

SOME TOADS CAN DETECT **EARTHQUAKES** BEFORE THEY HAPPEN.

When glass breaks, the cracks move

faster than

3,000 miles
an hour. (4,800 km/h)

A **SEA OTTER** HAS A **MILLION HAIRS** ON **ONE SQUARE INCH** (6.5 sq cm) **OF ITS BODY.**

EXTRACTS FROM HUMAN HAIR ARE USED TO MAKE SOME PIZZA CRUSTS.

The *Agathidium vaderi* **slime-mold beetle is named after Darth Vader because of its shiny, helmet-like head.**

The **dwarf gecko,** one of the world's tiniest **lizards,** can fit on your **fingernail.**

The **dot** over the letters **i** and **j** is called a **tittle.**

THERE ARE MORE
MOBILE
DEVICES
connected to the
WEB
THAN THERE ARE PEOPLE
LIVING ON EARTH.

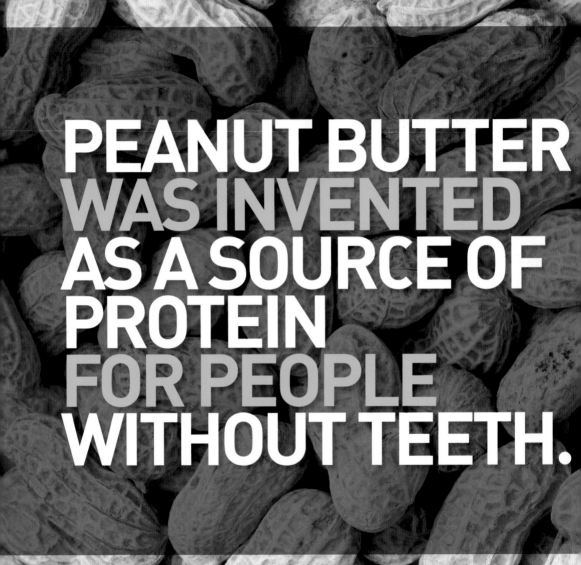

PEANUT BUTTER WAS INVENTED AS A SOURCE OF PROTEIN FOR PEOPLE WITHOUT TEETH.

It takes **540 peanuts** to make one 12-ounce (340-g) **jar** of peanut butter.

DRIBBLED A
BASKETBALL
FOR

230
(370 km) MILES

TO RAISE
MONEY
FOR JAPANESE
TSUNAMI
VICTIMS.

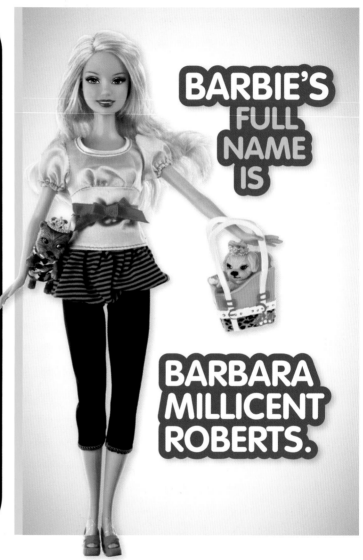

BARBIE'S
FULL
NAME
IS

BARBARA
MILLICENT
ROBERTS.

A LEOPARD WITH A STRAWBERRY-COLORED COAT WAS SPOTTED IN SOUTH AFRICA.

JIGSAW PUZZLES WERE ONCE CALLED "DISSECTED MAPS."

A WALRUS **TUSK** CAN GROW TO BE AS LONG AS A **BOOGIE BOARD.**

SOME PEOPLE
HIRE GOATS
TO MOW
THEIR LAWNS.

Some **cobras** can spit venom up to **6.5 feet—** (2 m) that's longer than a hockey stick!

AGOGGCHAUBUNAGUNGAMAUGG,
WORLD'S LONGEST NAME FOR A LAKE.

Your heart pumps enough blood in a day to fill 40 bathtubs.

IF YOU COUNTED ALL OF THE HOURS ANGRY BIRDS FANS HAVE SPENT PLAYING THE GAME, IT WOULD ADD UP TO MORE THAN ONE MILLION YEARS.

There is
no land on
Saturn.

You can buy **socks** made from **bamboo.**

A BLACK HOLE
CAN WEIGH AS MUCH AS
10 BILLION
SUNS.

IN MALAYSIA, PEOPLE TEXT "HA3" INSTEAD OF LOL.

A toy car—
dipped in **gold** and covered in **diamonds** and **rubies—**
sold for **$60,000** at a charity auction.

SCIENTISTS GREW PLANTS FROM 32,000-YEAR-OLD SEEDS.

YOUR RIGHT LUNG IS A LITTLE BIGGER THAN YOUR LEFT LUNG.

A rainbow looks different to every person who sees it.

YOU WILL LIKELY GET MORE THAN 600 COLDS IN YOUR LIFETIME.

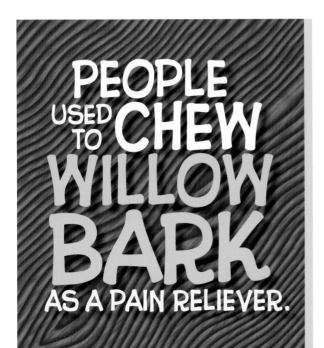

PEOPLE USED TO **CHEW** **WILLOW** **BARK** AS A PAIN RELIEVER.

Spider silk has been used to make **violin strings.**

56 MILLION YEARS AGO, **HORSES** WERE THE SIZE OF **HOUSE CATS.**

IN 2016,
CHINA
BUILT MORE
THAN TWICE
AS MANY
SKYSCRAPERS
AS THE NEXT
TEN COUNTRIES
COMBINED.

It's possible to **snow SKI** on the Big Island of Hawaii.

A RESTAURANT IN THE UNITED STATES BUILT A GIANT CORNED BEEF SANDWICH MADE OF

150 POUNDS OF MUSTARD (68 kg)
530 POUNDS OF LETTUCE (240 kg)
260 POUNDS OF CHEESE (118 kg)
1,032 POUNDS OF CORNED BEEF. (468 kg)

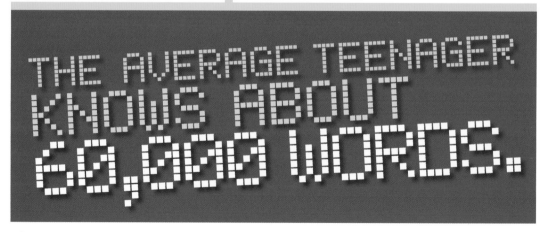

THE AVERAGE TEENAGER KNOWS ABOUT 60,000 WORDS.

THE TALLEST KNOWN
DINOSAUR,
SAUROPOSEIDON PROTELES,
WAS TALLER THAN A
SIX-STORY BUILDING.

A **giraffe**
sleeps
1½ hours a day.

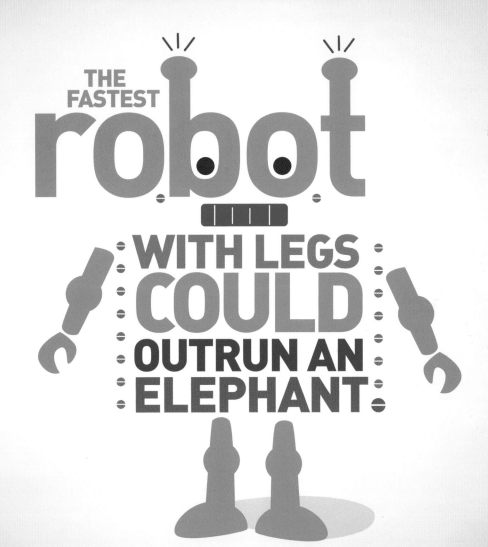

THE FASTEST **robot** WITH LEGS COULD OUTRUN AN ELEPHANT

THERE ARE OVER
A BILLION
MOTOR VEHICLES
ON THE **PLANET.**

There are more than 700 versions of the story of Cinderella.

A GROUP OF MUSICIANS IN CHINA MAKES **INSTRUMENTS** OUT OF SWEET POTATOES, CARROTS, AND OTHER **VEGETABLES.**

A BLUE WHALE'S LARGEST VEINS ARE SO BIG YOU COULD SWIM THROUGH THEM.

.There is a ski-up Starbucks at a ski resort IN THE UNITED STATES.

A GROUP OF **GREEN** anacondas **IS CALLED** A **BED.**

In 2007, A MAN SWAM THE ENTIRE LENGTH of the AMAZON RIVER— longer than the distance from NEW YORK CITY TO LOS ANGELES— IN **66** DAYS.

A FERRIS WHEEL in SHANGHAI, CHINA, is located on the ROOF of a SHOPPING MALL.

A STRAY DOG walked onstage and **SAT** by a **VIOLINIST** during an **ORCHESTRA CONCERT** in Ephesus, Turkey.

The mechanical **SHARKS** used in the 1975 movie **JAWS** were named **BRUCE.**

Some artists use **AVOCADO PITS AND FLESH** to create **ELABORATE ART.**

There is a **CHEMICAL ELEMENT** named after the **STATE OF CALIFORNIA.**

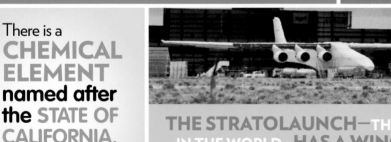

THE STRATOLAUNCH—**THE LARGEST AIRPLANE IN THE WORLD**—HAS A WINGSPAN LONGER THAN AN AMERICAN FOOTBALL FIELD.

BRITISH PRIME MINISTER **WINSTON CHURCHILL** WAS AN ACCOMPLISHED **ARTIST**.

SATURN'S MOON **ATLAS** looks like a FLYING SAUCER.

A NINE-YEAR-OLD BOY found a **1.2-MILLION**-YEAR-OLD **FOSSIL** by tripping over it.

That's Weird!

SCIENTISTS HAVE CREATED A **PATCH WITH 100 MINIATURE NEEDLES** THAT DISSOLVE INTO THE SKIN TO **DELIVER A FLU VACCINE**.

IN NEW ENGLAND, U.S.A., A **"JAKE"** IS AN **AFFECTIONATE TERM FOR A FIREFIGHTER**.

MAIL IS STILL DELIVERED BY MULE TO THE REMOTE TOWN OF SUPAI, ARIZONA, U.S.A.

SOMEONE TRIED TO SELL A CHICKEN McNUGGET SHAPED LIKE GEORGE WASHINGTON'S HEAD ON eBAY FOR $8,100.

CHICKENS
WITH WHITE EARLOBES
LAY WHITE
EGGS;
CHICKENS
WITH RED EARLOBES
LAY BROWN
EGGS.

One **ostrich egg**
is equal to
two dozen
chicken eggs.

**ABOUT
ONE IN A THOUSAND EGGS
HAS A DOUBLE YOLK.**

A restaurant on a Spanish island is built on top of a **volcano**— and uses a volcanic hole as a grill!

The Atlas **moth** has a **wingspan** as wide as a **toaster.**

SOME FRUIT DRINKS GET THEIR **PINK COLOR** FROM THE **EXTRACT OF COCHINEAL BUGS.**

THE LEAVES OF A CERTAIN **PALM TREE** CAN GROW TO BE AS LONG AS TWO STRETCH LIMOS.

A CAT USES **TINY HOOKS** ON ITS **TONGUE** LIKE A **HAIRBRUSH** DURING GROOMING.

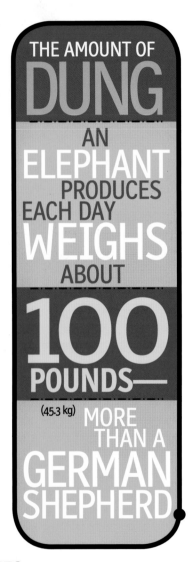

THE AMOUNT OF **DUNG** AN **ELEPHANT** PRODUCES EACH DAY **WEIGHS** ABOUT **100 POUNDS**— (45.3 kg) MORE THAN A **GERMAN SHEPHERD**.

Rats are ticklish

A helicopter engine is about the size of a backpack.

AN EXCITED
GUINEA
PIG
JUMPS
STRAIGHT
UP.

You
can buy
insurance
that covers
alien
abductions.

THE
SCARLET
IBIS
GETS ITS COLOR FROM THE
RED
CRABS
IT EATS.

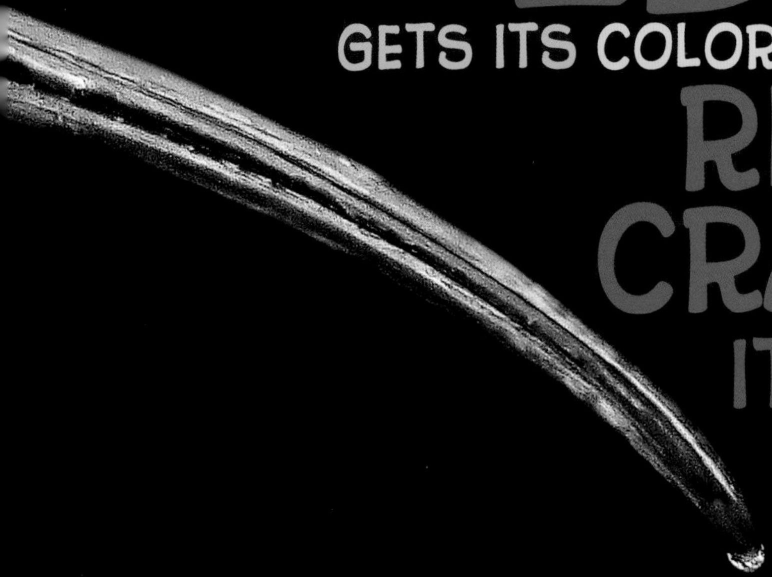

One in 1,000 people can't smell a skunk's spray.

THAT'S WEIRD!

SOME PEOPLE WHO HAVE LOST A LIMB CAN STILL FEEL IT.

Moondust **smells** like burnt gunpowder.

IT TAKES 6 MINUTES TO MAKE A MARSHMALLOW PEEP.

More people live in the Tokyo, Japan, **metro area than** in all of Canada.

IT TAKES ABOUT 460 GALLONS OF WATER (1,741 L) **TO MAKE ONE HAMBURGER.**

You can buy **cupcakes** through **24-hour** **ATMs.**

CLOUDS FORM LOWER IN THE SKY THAN THEY USED TO.

TREES WITH SQUARE TRUNKS GROW IN PANAMA.

There's a foam replica of Stonehenge in Virginia, U.S.A.

One out of every **10,000** clovers is a four-leaf clover.

BABIES BLINK ONLY ONCE OR TWICE EVERY MINUTE— ADULTS BLINK 10 to 15 TIMES.

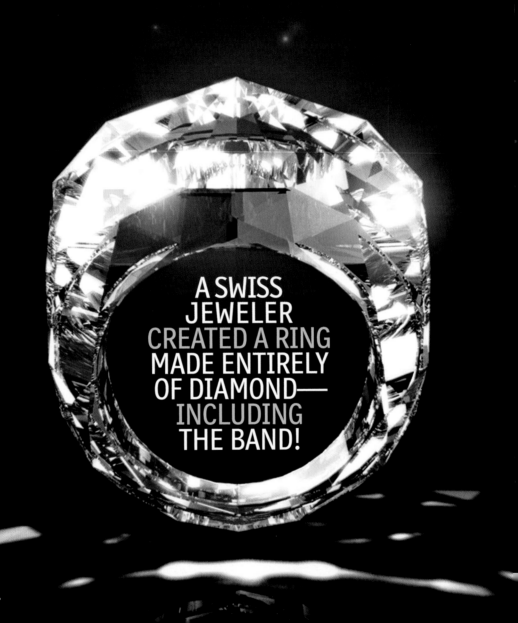

A SWISS JEWELER CREATED A RING MADE ENTIRELY OF DIAMOND—INCLUDING THE BAND!

In China you can buy green tea cream–flavored Oreo cookies.

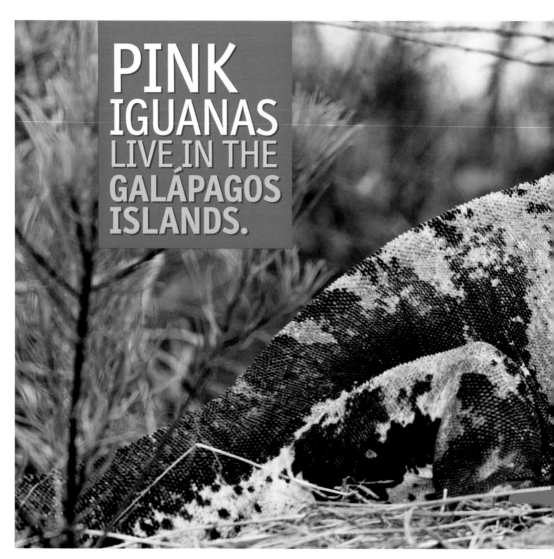

PINK
IGUANAS
LIVE IN THE
GALÁPAGOS
ISLANDS.

People who fear numbers suffer from arithmophobia.

ISTANBUL, TURKEY, IS LOCATED ON TWO CONTINENTS:

EUROPE

ASIA

EUROPE AND ASIA.

A
squid
can change
its color and pattern
in 700 milliseconds—
almost in the
blink of an eye.

The village of **Tilt Cove** in Newfoundland, Canada, has a population of

4

In the future, you may be able to take a space elevator **thousands of miles above Earth.**

The technical term for the **pound sign** on a phone is **octothorpe.** #

THE TEN MOST VENOMOUS **SNAKES** IN THE **WORLD** LIVE IN AUSTRALIA.

A **two-pound truffle** (0.9 kg) a rare mushroom— once sold for more than **$300,000.**

The first bicycles didn't have pedals.

ONE IN
1,461
PEOPLE ARE
BORN ON
LEAP
DAY.

The Olympic flame travels with its own guards.

AS YOU TRAVEL CLOSER TO THE SPEED OF LIGHT TIME SLOWS DOWN.

A DUTCH COMPANY HAS MADE A **FLYING** THREE-WHEELED CAR THAT CAN REACH **112 miles an hour** (180 km/h) ON LAND OR IN THE AIR.

THERE ARE NO RIVERS IN SAUDI ARABIA.

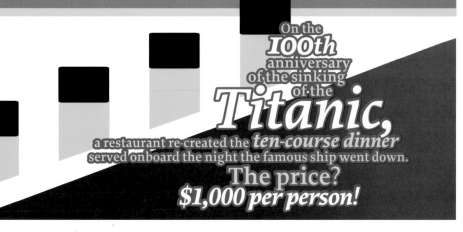

On the **100th** anniversary of the sinking of the *Titanic,* a restaurant re-created the *ten-course dinner* served onboard the night the famous ship went down. **The price?** *$1,000 per person!*

SCHNAUZER + POODLE

SCHNOODLE

THE WORLD'S LARGEST **GARDEN GNOME** IS TALLER THAN A GIRAFFE.

WORLD FAMOUS GNOME
NANOOSE BAY ESSO

THE **JACKFRUIT**— THE LARGEST FRUIT THAT GROWS ON A TREE— CAN WEIGH UP TO **110 POUNDS.** (50 kg) THAT'S THE WEIGHT OF 293 APPLES!

Some **artists** _in Mexico_ **paint portraits** _on baked_ **tortillas.**

TULIP BULBS WERE ONCE USED AS A KIND OF **CURRENCY** IN **HOLLAND.**

There's a **snail** that floats by making a **bubbly raft** out of its mucus.

YOU MAY SPEND UP TO HALF OF YOUR WAKING HOURS DAYDREAMING, ACCORDING TO ONE STUDY.

GUESS WHAT?

Your tongue would reach down to your belly button if you were a _____!
WHAT?

Ladybugs sometimes play pretend!
WHEN?

Hot water freezes faster than cold water!
WHY?

WANNA FIND OUT?

The FUN doesn't have to end here! Find these far-out facts and more in *Weird But True! 5*.

NATIONAL GEOGRAPHIC KiDS

That's Weird!

NATIONAL GEOGRAPHIC KIDS

weird but true! 5

350 OUTRAGEOUS FACTS

FACTFINDER

Boldface indicates illustrations.

A

A (letter) 76
Aberdeen, Washington, U.S.A. 117
Afghanistan 76
Agathidium vaderi 134
Airplanes 71, **71**, 121, 164, **164**
Alarm clocks 62, **62**
Alaska: earthquakes 8
Aliens 173, **173**
Amazon River, South America 164
Amnesia 65
Angry Birds (video game) 146
Antarctica 14, 124
Anteaters **86–87**, 87
Ants 12, 36, 88, **88**
Apollo 8 94
Apples 109
Apps 125
Arithmophobia 188
Asteroid Day 44
Astronauts 59, 63, **63**, 108
Atlas (moon) 165, **165**
Atlas moths 170
ATMs 44, 178, **178**
Australia
    deserts **104–105**, 105
    poisonous snakes 194
    prehistoric bird 8
    rock concert for dogs 12
Avatar (movie) 78, **78–79**
Avocados 164, **164**
Azerbaijan 76

B

Babies 183, **183**
Bacteria 27
Bahamas 82, **82**
Balloons 39, **39**, 108
Bamboo **148–149**, 149
Bananas 52, **52**, 109
Barbie (doll) 138, **138**
Baseball 44, **44**, 53
Basketball 85, **85**, 116, **116–117**, 118, 138
Bats 24, **24**, 32, 53
Beaches **54–55**, 82, **82**
Beavers 32, 100
Bees 27
Beetles 58, 134
Bicycles 37, 195
Bigfoot 72, **72–73**
Black holes 150
Black lights 52, **52**
Bladders, full 115
Blinking 183
Blood 36, 119, 145
Blue (color)
    bananas 52, **52**
    lobsters 15, **15**
    stork 27, **27**
    sunglasses 112, **112**
Blue whales 163
Body parts, artificial 124, **124**
Bones 16, **16–17**, 83, 94, 106
Box jellyfish 14
Brain 14, **14**, 91, 102
Brain freeze 43
Bridges 57, **57**, 84, **84**
Brooklyn Bridge, New York City, U.S.A. 84, **84**
Butter 103
Buttons 102, **102**

C

California, U.S.A.
    deep-fried Kool-Aid 7, **7**
    element named after 164
    robber wearing socks on hands 84
    tiny puppy 74, **74**
Camels 109, **109**
Carrots 118, **118**, 163, **163**
Cars 45, **55**, 121, **160–161**, 197, **197**
Caterpillars 47, **47**
Catfish 43, **43**
Cats 125, **125**, **153**, 171, **171**
Cell phones 37
Centipedes 85
Chalk 38, **38**
Chargoggagoggmanchauggagog-gchaubunagungamaugg, Lake, Massachusetts, U.S.A. 144–145

FACTFINDER

FACTFINDER

FACTFINDER

PHOTOCREDITS

Published by National Geographic Partners, LLC.
All rights reserved. Reproduction of the whole
or any part of the contents without written
permission from the publisher is prohibited.

Since 1888, the National Geographic Society has
funded more than 12,000 research, exploration,
and preservation projects around the world.
The Society receives funds from National
Geographic Partners, LLC, funded in part by
your purchase. A portion of the proceeds from
this book supports this vital work. To learn
more, visit natgeo.com/info.

For more information, visit
nationalgeographic.com, call 1-877-873-6846,
or write to the following address:

National Geographic Partners
1145 17th Street N.W.
Washington, D.C. 20036-4688 U.S.A.

Visit us online at nationalgeographic.com/books

For librarians and teachers:
ngchildrensbooks.org

More for kids from National Geographic:
natgeokids.com

For information about special discounts
for bulk purchases, please contact National
Geographic Books Special Sales:
specialsales@natgeo.com

For rights or permissions inquiries, please
contact National Geographic Books Subsidiary
Rights: bookrights@natgeo.com

Designed by Rachael Hamm Plett, Moduza Design

First edition published 2012
Reissued and updated 2018

Trade paperback: 978-1-4263-3110-7
Reinforced library binding ISBN:
978-1-4263-3111-4

The publisher would like to thank Jen Agresta,
project manager; Robin Terry, project manager;
Julie Beer, researcher; Michelle Harris,
researcher; Sarah Wassner Flynn, project
editor; Paige Towler, project editor; Eva
Absher-Schantz, art director; Julide Dengel,
art director; Kathryn Robbins, art director;
Ruthie Thompson, designer; Lori Epstein,
photo director; Hillary Leo, photo editor;
Alix Inchausti, production editor; Anne
LeongSon and Gus Tello, production assistants.

Printed in China
19/PPS/3